The Overdraft Trap:

How to Fight Back Against Predatory Banking

First published by Aussie Trading LLC

Library of Congress Catalog
Names: Rodulfo, Juan
ISBN: 979-8-2409-3853-5 (e-book)
ISBN: 979-8-2409-3854-2 (paperback)
ISBN: 979-8-2409-3855-9 (hardcover)
First edition
Layout by Juan Rodulfo
Cover art by Guaripete Solutions
Production: Aussie Trading, LLC
books@aussietrading.ltd
Printed in the USA

“"My journey into the overdraft trap taught me a harsh and unforgiving lesson: these aren't just benign 'fees.' They are meticulously placed financial landmines, strategically designed to detonate when you're at your most vulnerable."”

Juan Rodulfo

Introduction: The shocking reality

Every year, American banks extract over $12 billion in overdraft fees from their customers. Let that number sink into twelve billion dollars. This is not just an unfortunate consequence of financial mismanagement; it is a meticulously designed system, often preying on the most vulnerable among us — the everyday workers -, the gig economy hustlers, the families striving to make ends meet. This is not an accident. This is a trap.

You might be reading this because you have felt the sting of an unexpected fee, watched your balance dwindle into the negative, or felt that sickening lurch when your card gets declined despite your best efforts. You might feel frustrated, embarrassed, or even stupid. You are not alone. And more importantly, it is not your fault.

This book is your arsenal. It is a journey from confusion to clarity, from helplessness to empowerment. We will expose how these predatory systems work, equip you with the knowledge and tools to fight back, and show you how to build a financial future where your money works for you, not for the insatiable appetite of distant shareholders.

My name is Juan Rodulfo, and I know this trap intimately. I have walked that tightrope, watched the fees pile up, and ultimately, found a way to not just survive, but to reclaim my financial dignity. This is not just my story; it is a call to action for anyone who has ever felt frustrated by their bank, and for every advocate committed to a fairer financial world. It is time to stop being the prey. It is time to fight back.

Part 1: The Trap – My Story & The Human Cost

Chapter 1: The Bounce – When the System Broken

April 2026. Another day, another grind under the relentless sun of the gig economy. My mornings began religiously at 6:30 AM: a quick coffee, a modest piece of cake, then the familiar glow of three different apps firing up on my phone. Each click, each swipe, was a gamble. Every mile driven in my car, constantly threatened with repossession, was a desperate hope for a decent delivery, a run that might push my daily earnings past the $50 mark, maybe even reaching that rare, almost mythical $120 'summer solstice' income. My wife and I were already behind on rent, navigating the awkward necessity of borrowing from family, and the pressure was a constant, suffocating weight.

I kept a meticulous mental ledger. With earnings that barely scraped into three figures on a good day, I had to know every cent. There was no room for error, no safety net. So, when I stood at the supermarket checkout, pushing a cart with a few essential groceries, I was confident. I had checked, I had calculated. The small total on the screen was well within what I expected to have. The cashier scanned the last item; I swiped my card...

And it bounced.

The word hung in the air, a public declaration of my financial precarity. My face flushed, not just with embarrassment, but with a visceral shock. Bounced? It could not be. I knew what was supposed to be there. This was not a simple miscalculation on my part; this felt like an attack.

Then, the sickening realization hit me like a cold wave. The bank. My bank. They had paid a payday loan I had taken out, siphoning the few precious dollars that should have covered my groceries. But they had not just paid it; they had over drafted my account in the process. It was not just a single transaction; it was the trigger. One single action by the bank, choosing to cover a loan and slap me with a fee, opened the floodgates. From that moment, a dark, insidious pattern began. My account, already teetering, was now plummeting into a chasm of fees, one piling on top of the other, for reasons that felt entirely beyond my control.

The card bouncing was not just an inconvenience; it was the chilling, unmistakable sound of the trap snapping shut. It was the moment I utterly understood that the system I relied on was not just broken, but actively working against me.

Chapter 2: The Grind – A Life Defined by Scarcity

Life as a gig economy driver is not just a job; it is a relentless calculation of survival, a treadmill where every step forward risks pushing you closer to the edge. My car, which was my office and my lifeline, was a constant source of anxiety, called to repossession every other day. My wife and I were barely making ends meet, relying on the strained generosity of family to cover overdue rent payments. The hope I started each day with—to snag some of those 'best paid deliveries'—was a fragile thing, often crushed by the reality of a meager $50 income, barely enough to keep the wheels turning.

The constant worry about my bank balance was not some abstract financial concern; it was physical weight, a suffocating presence that affected every aspect of my day. As I navigated traffic and rushed between deliveries, my mind was a battlefield of numbers. How much do I have? Will this delivery cover that bill? Is there another fee lurking to swallow what little I have earned? It was exhausting, a mental tax layered on top of the physical demands of driving.

There was no room for error, no capacity for an unexpected expense. Every cent had a destination, a purpose. If I made $100, twenty went straight into the gas tank to keep the engine running, another twenty for the bare necessities—snacks, breakfast, lunch on the go. What little remained went towards groceries on the way home. It was a cycle of constant, immediate allocation, with nothing left over.

This was not just about financial instability; it was about the insidious creep of desperation in every corner of my life. My evenings were often spent filling out applications for 8-to-5 jobs, only to face the same disheartening rejections, again and again. The dream of a steady paycheck, of financial predictability, felt like an impossible luxury.

The pressure forced me to make difficult, almost counter-intuitive choices. I could not trust the banking system that had just betrayed me. I simply stopped using those accounts or at least compartmentalized them with extreme prejudice.

My income flowed into one account, distinct from another used for expenses. It was a desperate, almost radical act of self-preservation, a conscious move to protect my dwindling resources from the constant threat of yet another predatory fee. This was not about convenience; it was about creating a fortress, however small, against a system that seemed intent on stripping me off every last cent.

Chapter 3: The Betrayal – When Trust Turns to Treachery

I had always operated under a fundamental, perhaps naive, assumption about banks: they were meant to be custodians of my money, a dependable partner in managing my finances. I understood the concept of an overdue payment penalty; that is the explicit contract. But to be charged over $300 in a single fee, or to watch an $8 'auto overdraft charge' transform into a daily, phantom limb amputating my dwindling funds? That was not a penalty. I felt ransacked. What does that even mean? It means they view my struggle not as a problem to be solved, but as an opportunity to extract maximum profit. It means they see my empty wallet as their gold mine, stripping away not just my money, but my dignity.

The initial shock quickly morphed into a profound sense of betrayal. The very institutions I entrusted with my livelihood were actively working against it. This was not just a breakdown in service; it was a violation of an implicit contract. I expected fairness, transparency, and at the very least, a system that did not deliberately push me into deeper debt. Instead, I faced what felt like a calculated strategy of extraction.

The final insult came not through the shouting matches I had learned to avoid by screening my calls, but through the sterile, corporate language of their correspondence. PNC's email, a polite invitation to 'talk,' felt like a calculated attempt to wear me down, to subtly shift the blame back onto me, even after I had already sent a formal, legally framed letter demanding accountability for what I considered their 'vandalic actions.' Their insistence on phone calls, despite my clear request for written communication, felt like another tactic of evasion, an attempt to gaslight me into accepting their narrative without a verifiable record.

And then there was the letter from First National Bank of Pennsylvania. It did not offer solutions or empathy; it offered justification. It was dense with banking jargon, a bureaucratic smokescreen designed to make me feel inadequate for not understanding their predatory practices. It was not an explanation; it was an insult. It reinforced the feeling that these banks saw me as a 'customer' to be managed, not a 'member' to be served.

I recall the moment at the PNC branch when the manager offered a 'courtesy' elimination of a mere 20% of the fees. A 'courtesy.' My accounts were still deep in a 'three-figure fees debt,' and this was their solution. I could not help but let out a hollow, ironic laugh. I thanked her for the 'courtesy' of not demanding the money the bank never earned, money I had literally sweated for, driving a hundred miles a day just to keep my head above water. It was not a gesture of goodwill; it felt like a robber giving back a few coins after ransacking your home. In that moment, the very idea of trust in a financial institution was shattered beyond repair. I felt utterly, unequivocally robbed.

Chapter 4: The Outrage – A Line in the Sand

The shock of the bounced card, the gnawing anxiety of the daily grind, the bitter taste of betrayal—it all coalesced into a single, burning outrage. I watched, horrified, as the fees stacked up: $35, then $70, then $105, even a staggering $350. Are you kidding me? My mind screamed the question. This was beyond punitive. There was no rationale, no reasonable explanation for such exorbitant charges, especially when my funds were already so tight. This was not just bad service; this was an active assault on my financial survival.

That was the turning point. The initial helplessness transformed into a fierce resolve. I could not simply stand by and allow these financial giants to bleed me dry. This was not just about my empty wallet anymore; it was about the fundamental injustice of a system designed to exploit the vulnerable. The thought of all those other drivers, other families, other small business owners caught in this exact same trap, feeling the same shame and desperation, fueled a new determination within me. Their stories, though unheard, echoed my own.

I remember thinking, 'If the banks won't treat me with dignity, if they refuse to acknowledge the human cost of their greed, then I will fight back with every tool at my disposal.' This was not just a personal battle; it felt like a call to arms. I realized that my voice, even if small, could be amplified by the sheer audacity of demanding what was right. The line had been drawn. I was no longer just a victim of the overdraft trap; I was a warrior emerging from its depths, ready to expose its mechanisms and, hopefully, help others find their own way out. The fight for my money, and for the financial dignity of countless others, had just begun.

Part 2: Unmasking the Beast – How the System Works Against You

Chapter 5: Decoding the Trap – Identifying the Fees That Bleed You Dry

My journey into the overdraft trap taught me a harsh and unforgiving lesson: these are not just benign 'fees.' They are meticulously placed financial landmines, strategically designed to detonate when you are at your most vulnerable. The bank statement, once a simple record, transformed into a scroll of ever-increasing dread, each line a fresh wound, a further assault on my dwindling resources. It is crucial to understand the names they give these financial extractions, because knowing your enemy is the absolute first step to defending yourself.

Here are the culprits I encountered directly, the charges that spiraled my accounts into chaos and cost me hundreds of dollars in a matter of weeks and months:

- **Overdraft Fee**: This is often the primary and most insidious culprit. It is levied when you attempt a transaction (like a debit card purchase, an ATM withdrawal, or a check) for more money than you currently have in your account. Instead of simply declining the transaction, the bank chooses to cover it – but not out of generosity. They cover it only to slap you with a hefty fee, typically ranging from $25 to $35 per transaction. For me, these were constant, relentless jabs, each one pushing my balance deeper into the red and making it harder to recover.

- **Auto Overdraft Charge**: This variation often feels like a stealth attack. Similar to the standard overdraft fee, but sometimes triggered by smaller, everyday transactions or automatic payments. The automated nature of these charges, often a consistent $8 as I experienced, lulls you into a false sense of security, making you believe the impact is minor, only for it to compound quickly. Each $8 charge felt like a direct taunt, a reminder that the system was constantly watching, waiting for the strike.
- **Surcharge Fee**: While there is not always an overdraft fee directly, these often appear when you are desperate for cash and use an out-of-network ATM. If you are already low on funds and trying to avoid an overdraft from your own bank, using a different ATM might incur a surcharge from that ATM operator, potentially pushing your account into overdraft territory with your own bank, leading to yet another fee. It is an additional layer of cost, catching you in an inconvenient situation.
- **Continuous Overdraft Fee** (or Extended Overdraft Fee): This is where the predatory nature truly reveals itself. This is not just a fee for an initial overdraft. This is a fee charged every few days that your account remains negative. The bank is not merely

penalizing you for a single instance of insufficient funds; they are penalizing you for not immediately bringing your account back to positive, even when their own fees are making that task virtually impossible. It creates a vicious, self-perpetuating cycle designed to keep you trapped, compounding the problem until your balance is terrifyingly deep in the red. This felt like a deliberate strategy to ensure escape was as difficult as possible.

These are not accidental charges; they are components of a sophisticated system of extraction. And when you see fees of $35, $70, $105, or even an overwhelming $350 piling up one on top of the other, for what felt like no reason at all, you realize this is not about covering a transaction. This is about taking money that does not belong to them. This is about profiting from your misfortune.

Chapter 6: The Illusion of Legality – Understanding Their Playbook

When confronted with such blatant abuse – the escalating fees, the deliberate drain on my funds – my gut reaction was not just anger, but a profound, unshakeable conviction: these actions must be illegal. Predatory. Abusive. How could a bank be allowed to simply seize money that was not theirs, money I had worked tirelessly for, and frame it as a 'fee'? To me, it was clear:

I felt like this was financial theft, and it demanded legal penalization by the state.

And while the banks might hide behind layers of fine print and complex regulations, the truth is, from a consumer's perspective, my conviction stands. Their actions, though often structured to skirt explicit illegality, are fundamentally unjust, exploitative, and often operate within regulatory grey areas that prioritize bank profit over consumer protection. Understanding these technicalities, even without becoming a legal scholar, is crucial to fighting back. It is about unmasking their playbook.

Here is how they often operate, and the principles they often violate:

- **The "Opt-In" Sham (Regulation E)**: For many debit cards purchases and ATM withdrawals, banks are supposed to obtain your explicit, affirmative consent – your 'opt-in' – before they can charge you an overdraft fee. Regulation E (12 C.F.R. § 1005.17) mandates this. The idea is simple: you should have a choice. Either the bank declines the transaction for insufficient funds with no fee, or they cover it only if you have agreed to pay the overdraft fee. In practice, this 'opt-in' is often buried in lengthy documents you sign when opening an account or presented in a way that makes declining seem less desirable. My experience taught me that if you have not given clear, affirmative consent for specific types of transactions, those fees are absolutely disputable. The bank needs to provide documentary evidence of your consent; if they cannot, they are on shaky ground.

- **Unfair, Deceptive, or Abusive Acts or Practices (UDAAP)**: This is a powerful consumer protection concept. Under the Dodd-Frank Wall Street Reform and Consumer Protection Act, financial institutions are prohibited from engaging in practices that are unfair, deceptive, or abusive (UDAAP). What does this mean in practice for overdrafts?

- *Unfair*: A practice is unfair if it causes substantial injury to consumers that they cannot reasonably avoid, and that is not outweighed by any countervailing benefits to consumers or competition. Charging cascading fees, or reordering transactions (see below) to maximize fees, can easily be argued as unfair.

- *Deceptive*: A practice is deceptive if it misleads or is likely to mislead a consumer, and that consumer's interpretation is reasonable. Hiding fee structures in fine print or not clearly explaining how fees are triggered can be deceptive.

- *Abusive*: A practice is abusive if it materially interferes with a consumer's ability to understand a term or condition of a financial product or service or takes unreasonable advantage of a consumer's lack of understanding or inability to protect their interests. Taking advantage of someone in a precarious financial situation through excessive fees is a prime example. My experience, with charges accumulating relentlessly when I was barely making ends meet, felt like a textbook case of abuse.

- **Breach of Contract and Duty of Good Faith and Fair Dealing**: When you open an account, you enter into a contract with your bank. This contract, under common law, includes an implied Duty of Good Faith and Fair Dealing. This means the bank must act honestly and reasonably, not exploit you for their own profit. When they intentionally create a system that traps you in endless fees or fail to properly credit a significant deposit (like my $620 Zelle payment) to prevent further fees, they are breaching this fundamental duty. They are acting as an adversary, not a partner.

- **The Posting Order Trick**: This is one of the most insidious ways banks maximize fees. Imagine you have $50 in your account. You make five $10 purchases, then one $60 purchase. If the bank processes the transactions in the order they occurred, only the $60 purchase would overdraft you, incurring one fee. But many banks will reorder transactions, often processing the largest transactions first. In this scenario, the $60 purchase would go through, over drafting you. Then, the remaining five $10 purchases would also overdraft, each incurring a separate fee. Suddenly, one overdraft becomes six, turning a manageable mistake into financial catastrophe. This manipulation is a clear illustration of their profit-driven playbook.

Understanding these basic tenets, even without becoming a legal expert, empowers you. It shifts the narrative from 'I made a mistake' to 'The bank committed an injustice.' This fundamental understanding is your shield against their 'gaslighting' and your sword in the fight for your money. It validates the burning outrage you feel – because their actions, in spirit and often in practice, are indeed predatory, abusive, and disrespectful.

Chapter 7: The Data Doesn't Lie

My story, with its bounced cards, cascading fees, and the profound sense of betrayal, might feel intensely personal. But the chilling truth is, it is not unique. My experience is a single thread in a vast tapestry of financial exploitation woven by the very institutions we are told to trust. The data does not lie; it screams.

Every year, banks in the United States collect billions of dollars in overdraft and non-sufficient funds (NSF) fees. While the exact figures fluctuate, reports from the Consumer Financial Protection Bureau (CFPB) and various financial analyses consistently show staggering amounts, often exceeding $10 to $15 billion annually. To put that into perspective, imagine a massive dam, and that sum is the constant, powerful flood of money flowing out of consumer accounts and directly into bank coffers, year after year.

Who is withstanding the worst of this financial extraction? It is not the wealthiest account holders with ample buffers. The data clearly indicates that overdraft fees disproportionately impact those who can least afford them:

- Low-income individuals and families: Those living paycheck to paycheck are far more likely to dip into negative balances, becoming trapped in the continuous overdraft cycle. For someone earning $50 a day, a single $35 fee represents nearly a full day's wages, forcing impossible choices between necessities.

- Gig economy workers and those with volatile incomes: Like me, many Americans rely on irregular income streams. The unpredictable nature of deposits and expenses makes them prime targets for overdrafts, as balancing an account becomes a constant, high-stakes gamble.

- Minority communities: Studies have shown that minority households are often more likely to face these fees, highlighting an underlying issue of financial inequality within the banking system.

Consider this: A bank typically incurs only a few cents, if anything, to process an overdraft. Yet, they charge $25, $30, or even $35 for this 'service.' That is an astronomical profit margin, far exceeding what would be considered reasonable in almost any other industry. This is not about covering costs; it is about maximizing revenue. It is about a business model built on the financial precarity of its customers.

Furthermore, the practice of reordering transactions to maximize fees, which we discussed in the previous chapter, is not just a theory; it is a documented tactic. While some regulatory efforts have been made, many banks continue to employ practices that prioritize their bottom line over the financial stability of their account holders. This means a single, small misstep can quickly snowball into dozens of dollars in fees, not because you made multiple large errors, but because the bank strategically processed your transactions to generate the most revenue possible.

When you look at these numbers, the anger I felt becomes a shared outrage. My personal experience was not an anomaly; it was a symptom of a deeply entrenched, predatory system. The data is a mirror, reflecting the struggles of millions, and it serves as a powerful call to action: you are not alone in this fight, and by understanding the scope of the problem, we can better arm ourselves to dismantle it.

Part 3: Fighting Back – Your Survival Guide

Chapter 8: Your AI Ally – How Technology Levels the Playing Field

When I realized the sheer scale of the fees and the bank's dismissive, almost 'gaslighting' responses, I knew I could not fight them with polite requests or desperate phone calls. I needed a legal voice, a formal avenue for my demands, but the reality of affording an attorney was a luxury I simply could not contemplate. My income, perpetually dancing on the edge of the overdraft trap, certainly did not stretch to legal fees.

That is when I turned to an unexpected ally: Artificial Intelligence. I transformed a readily available digital assistant into my personal legal advocate. This was not just about drafting a letter; it was about leveraging innovative technology to combat a Goliath with an institutional, well-funded legal advantage. It was about leveling the playing field.

The process was surprisingly straightforward and incredibly empowering. I used a large language model, a common AI tool, to craft my formal demand letters to both PNC Bank and First National Bank of Pennsylvania. My prompt to the AI was direct, assertive, and left no room for ambiguity. It was designed to pull together all the facts of my ordeal and present them in a language the banks would be forced to take seriously:

'Act as my personal attorney and write a strongly legal letter to PNC Bank requesting the devolution of all debits made since February 23, 2026 (attached bank statement), including overdraft fees to allow the availability of the Zelle payment received from customer XXXXXXXXXX made on March 3, 2026 for $620, making emphasis that all these overdraft fees have deeply harmed my business and me emotionally and personally, and asking not to overdraft the account in the future.'

I fed the AI the raw facts of my bank statement, highlighting specific dates, the exact amounts of the fees, and the critical detail of the $620 Zelle payment that should have unequivocally prevented further overdrafts. I emphasized the devastating impact these fees had on my business and, crucially, on me personally and emotionally. The AI took my lived experience, my mounting frustration, and my burning demand for justice, and translated it into the formal, legalistic language that banks understand.

The beauty of this approach is its accessibility. You do not need a law degree to draft a compelling legal argument. The AI cited relevant regulations, articulated the harm to my business and personal well-being, and laid out clear, non-negotiable demands for reimbursement and a cessation of future overdrafts.

This was not just an email; it was a formal notice of intent, a document that forced the bank to acknowledge the gravity of my complaint. It signaled that I was serious, that I understood my rights (even if I needed a digital assistant to help articulate them), and that I would not be easily dismissed.

This innovative use of technology transformed my personal battle into a blueprint for others. It was my way of saying, 'You will not dismiss me, and you will not win without a fight.' And it showed me that in this modern age, even the Davids of the financial world can find powerful slingshots to challenge the Goliaths.

Chapter 9: Dispute & Demand – Crafting Your Case

You have identified the fees, you understand how the system is designed to trap you, and you have seen how technology can empower your voice. Now, it is time to take concrete action. The goal is to formally dispute the charges and demand resolution. Remember, banks often rely on you giving up on you being too intimidated or exhausted to fight back. A well-crafted, formal letter cuts through the noise and forces them to take your complaint seriously.

The key to a successful dispute is to be clear, factual, and assertive, while maintaining a professional tone. You are not begging; you are demanding what is rightfully yours.

Here is a step-by-step guide to crafting your own dispute letter:

1. Gather Your Evidence: This is paramount. Collect every relevant bank statement showing the disputed fees, transaction histories, and any proof of deposits (like my Zelle payment) that should have prevented the overdrafts. Organize these documents chronologically.

2. Identify the Specific Fees and Dates: Go through your statements with a fine-tooth comb. List every single overdraft, NSF, or continuous overdraft fee, noting the exact date and amount of each. Also, identify the specific transactions that triggered these fees.

3. Reference Relevant Regulations (Even Generally): As we discussed in Chapter 6, knowing your basic rights is powerful. You do not need to quote legal code verbatim but referencing concepts like Regulation E (for opt-in requirements on debit/ATM overdrafts) or UDAAP (for unfair/abusive practices) adds weight to your claim. Your letter should imply that you understand their obligations.

4. State the Harm: Clearly articulate the financial and, if applicable, emotional distress these fees have caused. Do not be afraid to describe how these actions have disrupted your life, your business, or your ability to manage

basic necessities. This individualized touch reminds them of the human cost.

5. Demand Specific Actions: Be clear about what you want. Do you want a full refund of specific fees? A reversal of certain transactions? An immediate disabling of overdraft protection? State your demands unequivocally.

6. Set a Deadline: Give them a reasonable timeframe to respond, typically 10-15 business days. This shows you are serious and will escalate if necessary.

7. State Your Intent to Escalate: Clearly inform them of the next steps you will take if they fail to respond satisfactorily. This includes filing complaints with regulatory bodies like the Consumer Financial Protection Bureau (CFPB), the Office of the Comptroller of the Currency (OCC), or relevant state banking departments. Mentioning intent to seek legal remedies if necessary further underlines your resolve.

8. Send Via Certified Mail with Return Receipt: This is non-negotiable. Sending your letter this way provides you with irrefutable proof that the bank received your formal demand. This documentation is critical if you need to escalate your complaint later.

Template: Dispute Letter to Your Bank

[Your Name] [Your Address] [Your Phone Number] [Your Email Address]

[Date]

[Bank Name] Attn: Customer Advocacy / Dispute Resolution Department (or Legal Department) [Bank Address]

RE: Formal Demand for Reimbursement of Overdraft/NSF Fees and Cease of Overdraft Authorization Account Holder: [Your Full Name/Business Name] Account Number: [Your Account Number – Last 4 digits is often sufficient in the subject, full in body if needed]

To Whom It May Concern:

I am writing to formally dispute and demand the immediate reimbursement of all overdraft/non-sufficient funds ('NSF') fees and related charges assessed on my account [Your Account Number] from [Start Date of Fees] through the present date, including any pending transactions.

The following specific fees have been identified and are hereby formally disputed:

- [Date]: "[Type of Fee]" – $[Amount]
- [Date]: "[Type of Fee]" – $[Amount]
- [Date]: "[Type of Fee]" – $[Amount]
- (Continue listing all specific disputed fees and dates)

Total Amount in Dispute: $[Total Sum]

These charges, individually and collectively, constitute an excessive, unjustified, and often predatory financial burden. [Optionally, insert a brief sentence about the specific trigger, e.g., "This cascade of fees was triggered by the bank's processing of a payday loan, followed by a failure to properly apply a [Zelle/Direct Deposit] payment of $[Amount] received on [Date] that should have restored my account to a positive balance."]

Legal Basis for Dispute (choose applicable points):

This demand is grounded in applicable federal regulations and consumer protection principles, including but not limited to:

1. Regulation E (12 C.F.R. § 1005.17): To the extent overdraft fees were imposed on ATM

or one-time debit card transactions without my clear, affirmative, and informed opt-in consent. I request documentary evidence of such consent.

2. Unfair, Deceptive, or Abusive Acts or Practices (UDAAP): The repeated imposition of cascading overdraft fees, particularly in connection with low-dollar transactions and transaction posting practices, constitutes unfair and/or abusive conduct under federal law.

3. Breach of Contract and Duty of Good Faith and Fair Dealing: The systematic assessment of disproportionate fees, especially when account balances fluctuate due to the timing of deposits and withdrawals, violates the implied covenant of good faith and fair dealing.

Damages and Harm:

The overdraft fees assessed have caused significant and ongoing harm, including severe disruption to my cash flow, artificial inflation of negative balances due solely to fee accumulation, and considerable emotional distress, anxiety, and personal hardship.

Formal Demands:

Accordingly, I hereby demand that [Bank Name] take the following actions within ten (10) business days of your receipt of this letter:

1. Immediately reimburse the full amount of $[Total Sum], representing all disputed fees assessed from [Start Date of Fees] to date.

2. Provide a complete written accounting of all overdraft-related charges, including the triggering transactions and internal fee assessment methodology.

3. Provide documentary proof of valid opt-in consent for overdraft services, if any exists.

4. Immediately revoke and disable any overdraft protection or authorization and place my account in a 'decline-only' status to prevent any future overdraft transactions without my explicit, renewed, and documented authorization.

5. Confirm in writing that no further overdraft or NSF fees will be assessed absent explicit, renewed, and documented authorization.

Notice of Intent to Escalate:

If [Bank Name] fails to respond affirmatively and substantively to this demand within the stated timeframe, I hereby provide notice of my intent to:

1. File a formal complaint with the Consumer Financial Protection Bureau (CFPB) at consumerfinance.gov.

2. File a formal complaint with the Office of the Comptroller of the Currency (OCC) [if applicable to national banks].

3. File a formal complaint with the [Your State] Department of Banking and Securities [if applicable for state-chartered banks].

4. Pursue all available civil remedies in a court of competent jurisdiction.

5. Consider escalating this matter to media and consumer advocacy organizations to bring public attention to your overdraft fee practices.

This correspondence is submitted without prejudice to any rights, claims, or causes of action, all of which are expressly reserved.

I await your prompt and substantive written response no later than [Date - 10-15 business days from your sending date].

Respectfully submitted,

[Your Signature] [Your Typed Name] [Your Title/Capacity, e.g., "Account Holder" or "Authorized Representative"].

Chapter 10: The Alternative – Finding Sanctuary in Credit Unions

My disillusionment with commercial banks, born from their relentless fees and dismissive responses, led me to seek refuge in a fundamentally different kind of financial institution: the Credit Union. For far too long, I had been just a 'customer' to the big banks—a number on a spreadsheet, a 'cow to be leeched' for the benefit of distant, anonymous shareholders. The shift was not just about finding a new place to put my money; it was a profound psychological relief, a step towards reclaiming a sense of financial dignity that the commercial banking system had stripped away.

While the fundamental services offered—checking, savings, loans, debit cards—are outwardly similar to any other bank, the core difference lies in their mission and their very legal and financial structure. This distinction is critical:

Commercial Banks vs. Credit Unions: A Tale of Two Models

- Commercial Banks (like the ones that trapped me): These are for-profit corporations, publicly traded or privately owned, whose primary objective is to maximize profits for their shareholders. This profit motive often translates into aggressive fee structures, higher interest rates on loans, and a less personalized approach to customers. Your money is essentially their capital, which they use to finance a wide array of activities—some legal, some ethically questionable, across international markets—all designed to enrich those shareholders. You are a 'customer,' a revenue stream.

- Credit Unions: These are member-owned, non-profit financial cooperatives. This means that instead of having external shareholders, the people who bank there are the owners. Their primary objective is to serve their members, not to generate profit. Any "profits" or surplus funds are typically returned to members in the form of lower interest rates on loans, higher interest rates on savings, and significantly fewer, if any, predatory fees. The money you deposit is kept local, flowing back into the community and directly benefiting other members. You are a 'member,' a part of a collective.

The feeling of banking with a Credit Union is, therefore, fundamentally different. It is a relationship, a membership, built on mutual benefit rather than transactional exploitation. Their credit interest rates were far more affordable, a testament to their commitment to helping members rather than squeezing them for every cent. There's transparency, a sense of community, which is utterly absent in the cold, corporate halls of the big commercial banks.

Your money is not just sitting there; it is actively contributing to a system designed to uplift its participants.

Making the Switch:

Transitioning to a Credit Union is a powerful act of financial self-preservation. Here is how to start:

1. **Find a Credit Union**: Look for local credit unions in your area. Many also offer national membership if you meet certain criteria (e.g., specific affiliations, living in a certain community). Websites like MyCreditUnion.gov can help you locate options.
2. **Understand Membership Requirements**: Most credit unions have a common bond for membership (e.g., where you live, work, or organizations you belong to). These are typically easy to meet, or they might allow membership through a small donation to an associated charity.
3. **Open an Account**: Start with a small deposit to open a checking or savings account. Once established, you can begin the process of moving your direct deposits and automatic payments.
4. **Gradual Transition**: Do not move all your funds at once. Gradually shift your income and expenses to your new Credit Union account, ensuring all automatic payments and

direct deposits are successfully redirected before fully closing your old commercial bank account.

This shift was more than just moving funds; it was a defiant act against a system that had exploited me. It was about choosing an institution that valued me as a person, not as a source of revenue. It is about recognizing that you have a choice, and that choice can dramatically alter your financial landscape.

Chapter 11: Fortifying Your Finances – Strategies for the Gig Economy Warrior

Escaping the overdraft trap is not just about finding a better bank; it is about fundamentally rethinking how you manage your money, especially in the unpredictable landscape of the gig economy. The commercial banking system proved itself to be a predator, not a partner, and since you cannot trust it, you must build your own defenses.

My strategy is simple, yet fiercely effective: separate your financial life.

The Two-Account Firewall:

This method creates a crucial barrier between your hard-earned income and your outgoing expenses, providing a layer of protection against unexpected fees and miscalculations.

1. The Income Account (Your Fortress):

- **Purpose**: This account is solely for receiving your earnings from gig work, direct deposits, or any other income streams.
- **Recommendation**: As discussed in Chapter 10, I strongly recommend a Credit Union for this account. Their member-centric model provides a more secure and trustworthy environment for your primary financial intake.
- **Protection**: By keeping your income separate, you create a fortress. If an issue arises with an expense account, your main funds are protected in another institution. This allows you to breathe, to assess, and to make informed decisions without the immediate threat of your entire livelihood being compromised by cascading fees.
- **Access**: Limit direct spending from this account. Its primary function is to receive and hold your income until it is intentionally transferred to your expense account.

2. The Expenses Account (Your Disbursement Hub):

- **Purpose**: This account is where you pay all your bills, set up autopayments, and conduct your daily spending.
- **Recommendation**: This can be a commercial bank account or another credit union, depending on your preferences. The key is its separation from your primary income.
- **Risk Isolation**: The benefit here is crucial: if it happens that you miss an autopayment, and the bank gets 'crazy charging/over drafting you,' your core income remains protected in your separate institution. You isolate the risk, preventing one financial misstep from cascading into total ruin across all your funds.
- **Funding**: Fund this account with specific, predetermined amounts from your income account, timed to cover your upcoming bills and planned pending. This conscious transfer gives you more control and visibility.

This two-account strategy is your armor in the fight against financial vulnerability. It allows you to maintain control, isolate risk, and breathe a little easier knowing your hard-earned income is not constantly exposed to predatory fees.

Minimalism & Conscious Spending: Rejecting the Consumerist Trap

Beyond the mechanics of managing accounts, a deeper shift is required: a conscious rejection of the relentless consumerist pressure that drains your funds. 'Do not fall for stuff you do not need.' This became my mantra, a shield against the endless marketing designed to separate you from your money. Every business on this planet is trying to get the few cents you keep in your pockets, because those cents, when put together, become real money with time and low effort for them.

For me, it meant a radical re-evaluation of my spending habits, a return to fundamental needs:

- **Clothing**: Prioritize durability, function, and necessity over fleeting fashion trends. A new outfit might offer a momentary high, but it will not pay your rent or shield you from a predatory bank fee.

- **New Cellphones**: Resist the constant urge to upgrade. If your cellphone carrier is offering you the latest iPhone for a 'stupid' monthly payment of $35, take that money and invest it instead. Keep your current phone; it still works. The latest model is a status symbol, not a necessity.

- **TV Subscriptions & Junk Food**: Scrutinize every recurring expense and impulsive purchase. Do you genuinely need every streaming service? Is that daily fast-food habit serving your financial health? These small, often unconscious drains accumulate rapidly.

This is not about deprivation; it is about empowerment. Every dollar saved by resisting these consumerist urges is a dollar reclaimed, a tiny victory against the forces that want to keep your pockets perpetually empty. It allows you to 'save for days like today' – to build that crucial emergency fund that provides a real safety net, especially in the volatile gig economy. By controlling your outflow, you begin to take back the power.

Chapter 12: Becoming an Investor – Turning the Tables on the Exploiters

The most profound lesson I learned from being 'leeched' by the banking system and the consumerist machine is this: every business on this planet is trying to get the few cents you keep in your pockets. Why? Because those cents, when put together, become into real money with time and low effort for them. The banks profit from your misfortune, corporations profit from your impulses. They understand the power of aggregation and compounding better than anyone. The solution is simple, yet revolutionary: we must copy their strategy.

This is where investing, even starting with exceedingly tiny amounts, becomes a powerful and accessible act of financial liberation. It is a fundamental step toward long-term resilience and a direct counter to the feeling of being perpetually exploited. Instead of letting banks or corporations extract value from your money, you can put your money to work for you.

Investing: From $10 to Financial Freedom

The old notion that investing is only for the wealthy or financially sophisticated is a lie perpetuated by a system that benefits from your exclusion. Modern financial technology has democratized access to the markets. Platforms like Robin Hood App are just one example that allows you to invest from as little as $10.

Consider your conscious spending choices, as discussed in the previous chapter. That $35 monthly payment for the latest iPhone you do not truly need. Divert it. Put that money directly into your investment app. The same goes for money saved by cutting down on junk food, unused subscriptions, or impulsive clothing purchases. These small, consistent contributions can accumulate into something significant over time. This is magic. When your investments earn returns, those returns then earn returns themselves. Over time, even small, consistent investments can grow exponentially. This is the very engine that enriches shareholders of big banks and corporations – and it can be your engine too.

Why Invest? The Power of ETFs and Compounding

- ETFs (Exchange Traded Funds): Instead of trying to pick individual stocks, which can be risky, ETFs allow you to invest in a diversified basket of stocks, bonds, or other assets with a single purchase. This provides broad market exposure, reducing risk and often requiring less active management. It is a smart way for beginners to start.
- Compounding: This is the magic. When your investments earn returns, those returns then earn returns themselves. Over time, even small, consistent investments can grow exponentially. This is the very engine that enriches shareholders of big banks and corporations – and it can be your engine too.

Reclaiming Your Blood: A Long-Term Vision

This strategy—consciously saving and consistently investigates how you actively counteract the feeling of being 'leeched.' You redirect the flow. You keep your 'blood' – your hard-earned capital and its potential for growth – within your own system, for your own benefit and for the benefit of those you love. It transforms you from a passive victim into an active participant, an owner, rather than just a perpetual consumer.

It is about understanding that the same principles of aggregation and compounding that enrich the shareholders of huge corporations can, and should, enrich you. It is about taking that fundamental control over your financial destiny, moving beyond mere survival, and building a future where you are the one profiting from smart financial decisions, not the victim of predatory practices. This is the ultimate act of reclaiming your economic power and achieving true financial resilience.

Conclusion: Join the Movement – Reclaiming Our Financial Future

My journey through the overdraft trap began with a moment of profound public embarrassment, a bounced card in a supermarket aisle that quickly escalated into a financial nightmare. I felt the suffocating pressure of the gig economy, the sting of betrayal from institutions I was supposed to trust, and the burning outrage of watching my hard-earned money disappear into a vortex of predatory fees. It was a journey from feeling helpless to understanding the insidious mechanisms designed to exploit, and finally, to finding a fierce resolve to fight back.

This book has been more than just my story; it has been a roadmap. We have unmasked the specific fees that bleed accounts dry, dissected the banking playbook that hides exploitation behind technicalities, and validated the deep conviction that these practices are, at their core, unjust and predatory. More importantly, we have armed you with a survival guide: how to leverage technology to demand accountability, how to find sanctuary in member-owned credit unions, how to fortify your finances through strategic account separation and conscious spending, and how to turn the tables by becoming an investor, even with small amounts.

But this fight, while deeply personal, is not one to be waged alone. The data does not lie billions of dollars are siphoned annually from the pockets of those who can least afford it, disproportionately impacting vulnerable communities.

This is a systemic issue, and systemic issues demand collective action.

Join the Movement: Reclaiming Our Financial Future

This is a call to arms for anyone who has ever felt frustrated, exploited, or betrayed by their bank. Your individual actions, when multiplied by thousands, by millions, become an unstoppable force for change. It is time to transform our collective anger into a powerful, unified movement against predatory banking practices.

Here is how you can be a part of this movement:

1. Be an Informed Advocate: Use the knowledge gained from this book. Understand your rights, identify predatory fees, and never hesitate to challenge them using formal dispute processes, leveraging AI as your ally.

2. Choose Your Financial Allies Wisely: Move your money from institutions that exploit to those that serve. Embrace credit unions and ethical financial service providers. Every dollar you transfer is a vote for a fairer system.

3. Spread the Word: Share your story, share this book, share the knowledge. Talk to your friends, family, and colleagues about the overdraft trap. The more people who understand how they are being exploited, the weaker the exploiters become.

4. Demand Policy Change: Support consumer advocacy organizations that are fighting for stronger regulations against predatory banking practices. Contact your elected officials; tell them your story and demand legislation that protects consumers, limits exorbitant fees, and promotes financial fairness.

5. Become an Owner, Not Just a Consumer: Adopt the mindset of an investor. By saving and channeling even insignificant amounts into investment accounts, you redirect the flow of wealth, keeping your 'blood' in your own system. You become part of the solution, building your own financial resilience while undermining the very foundations of predatory wealth accumulation.

The fight for financial dignity is ongoing. It is a marathon, not a sprint. But armed with knowledge, empowered by technology, and united in purpose, we can challenge the Goliaths of the banking world. We can dismantle the overdraft trap. We can reclaim our financial future, not just for ourselves, but for generations to come. Let us make sure that no one else has to feel the humiliation of a bounced card or the crushing weight of unfair fees. The power to change this system lies with us. Let us use it.

The United States is the wealthiest nation in history, but its riches are concentrated in the hands of a tiny elite. It is time to reimagine equity, reclaim our democracy, and abolish billionaires for good.

The Author

Juan Ramon Rodulfo Moya, **Defined by Nature**: Inhabitant of Planet Earth, Human, Son of Eladio Rodulfo and Briceida Moya, Brother of Gabriela, Gustavo and Katiuska, Father of Gabriel and Sofia; **Defined by society**: Venezuelan Citizen (Limited Human Rights by default), Friend of many, enemy of few, Neighbor, Student/Teacher/Student, Worker/Supervisor/Manager/Leader/Worker, Husband of K/Ex-Husband of K/Husband of Y; **Defined by the U.S. Immigration Office**: Legal Alien; **Classroom studies**: Master's Degree in Human Resource Management, English, Mandarin Chinese; **Real-World Studies**: Human Behavior; **Home Studios**: SEO Webmaster, Graphic Design, Application and Website Development, Internet and Social Media Marketing, Video Production, YouTube Branding, Part 107 Commercial Drone Pilot, Import-Export, Affiliate Marketing, Cooking, Laundry, Home Cleaning; **Work experience**: Public-Private-Entrepreneurial Sectors; **Other definitions:** Bitcoin Evangelist, Human Rights, Peace and Love Advocate.

Publications:

Books:

Why Maslow? How to use his theory to stay in Power Forever (2018)
¿Por qué Maslow? Cómo usar su teoría para permanecer en el Poder por siempre (2018)
Asylum Seekers (2018)
En busca de Asilo (2018)
Manual for Gorillas: 9 Rules to be the "FER-PECT" dictator (2019)
Manual para Gorilas: 9 Reglas para ser el dictador "FER-PECTO" (2019)
Why you must Play the Lottery (2019)
Por qué debes jugar la Lotería (2021)
Para Español Oprima #2: Speaking Spanish in Times of Xenophobia (2019)
Cause of Death: IGNORANCE, Human Behavior in Times of PANIC (2019)
Politics explained for Millennials, GENs XYZ and future generations (2022)
Política explicada para Millennials, GENs xyz y futuras generaciones (2022)
Las cenizas del Ejército Libertador (2023)
Remain Silent: The only right we have. The legal Aliens (2023)
Fortune Cookie Coaching 88 Motivational Tips Made of Fortune Cookies, Vol I (2024)
Vicky Erotic Tales, Vol I (2024)
TikTok Heroes in my Algorithm (2025)

AI at Home, transforming your child's Learning Experience (2025)
IA en Casa, Reinventando el aprendizaje de l@s niñ@s (2025)
Self-made billionaire in the US, Girl, hold my beer (2025)

Blogs:

Noticias de Nueva Esparta, Ubuntu Café, Coffee Secrets, Rodulfox, Red Wasp Drone, Barista Pro, Gorila Travel, Fortune Cookie Coach, All Books, Vicky Toys.

Audiovisual Productions:

Podcasts:

Ubuntu Cafe | Vicky Erotic Tales | Fortune Cookie Coach | All Books, available at: juanrodulfo.com/podcasts

Music:

Albums: Margarita | Race to Extinction | Relaxed Panda | Amazonia | Cassiopeia | Caracas | Arcoiris Musical | Close Your Eyes, available at: juanrodulfo.com/music

Photography & Video:

On sale at Adobe Stock, iStock, Shutterstock, and Veectezy, available at: juanrodulfo.com/gallery

Social Media Profiles:

BlueSky / Twitter / FB / Instagram / TikTok/ VK / LinkedIn / Sina Weibo: @rodulfox

Google Author: https://g.co/kgs/grjtN5
Google Artist: https://g.co/kgs/H7Fiqg
Twitter: https://twitter.com/rodulfox
Facebook: https://facebook.com/rodulfox
LinkedIn: https://www.linkedin.com/in/rodulfox
Instagram: https://www.instagram.com/rodulfox/
VK: https://vk.com/rodulfox
TikTok: https://www.tiktok.com/@rodulfox
Trading View: https://www.tradingview.com/u/rodulfox/

Table of Contents

Appendices

Appendix A Bank Statements

6/8/26, 2:17 PM Account Activity

Account Activity

GUARIPETE ******1751

Balances as of	Available Balance:	Ledger Balance:
6/8/2026	($915.67)	($915.67)

Transactions

Date	Description	Category	Check	Deposits	Withdrawals
6/5/2026	Auto Overdraft Charge	UNCATEGORIZED			($8.00)
6/4/2026	Auto Overdraft Charge	UNCATEGORIZED			($8.00)
6/3/2026	Auto Overdraft Charge	UNCATEGORIZED			($8.00)
6/2/2026	Auto Overdraft Charge	UNCATEGORIZED			($8.00)
6/1/2026	Auto Overdraft Charge	UNCATEGORIZED			($8.00)
5/29/2026	Auto Overdraft Charge	UNCATEGORIZED			($8.00)
5/28/2026	Auto Overdraft Charge	UNCATEGORIZED			($8.00)
5/27/2026	Auto Overdraft Charge	UNCATEGORIZED			($8.00)
5/26/2026	Auto Overdraft Charge	UNCATEGORIZED			($8.00)
5/22/2026	Auto Overdraft Charge	UNCATEGORIZED			($8.00)
5/21/2026	Auto Overdraft Charge	UNCATEGORIZED			($8.00)
5/20/2026	Auto Overdraft Charge	UNCATEGORIZED			($8.00)
5/19/2026	Auto Overdraft Charge	UNCATEGORIZED			($8.00)
5/18/2026	Auto Overdraft Charge	UNCATEGORIZED			($8.00)
5/15/2026	Auto Overdraft Charge	UNCATEGORIZED			($8.00)
5/14/2026	Auto Overdraft Charge	UNCATEGORIZED			($8.00)
5/13/2026	Auto Overdraft Charge	UNCATEGORIZED			($8.00)
5/12/2026	Auto Overdraft Charge	UNCATEGORIZED			($8.00)
5/12/2026	OVERDRAFT FEE	UNCATEGORIZED			($35.00)
5/11/2026	Auto Overdraft Charge	UNCATEGORIZED			($8.00)
5/11/2026	OVERDRAFT FEE	UNCATEGORIZED			($70.00)
5/8/2026	Auto Overdraft Charge	UNCATEGORIZED			($8.00)
5/7/2026	Auto Overdraft Charge	UNCATEGORIZED			($8.00)

https://banking-fnb.fnb-onlinebankingcenter.com/FNBPA/Accounts/PMMActivity.aspx?Index=2 1/2

Figure 1. Bank Statement

6/8/26, 2:17 PM Account Activity

Date	Description	Category	Check	Deposits	Withdrawals
5/6/2026	Auto Overdraft Charge	UNCATEGORIZED			($8.00)
5/6/2026	OVERDRAFT FEE	UNCATEGORIZED			($35.00)
5/5/2026	Auto Overdraft Charge	UNCATEGORIZED			($8.00)
5/5/2026	OVERDRAFT FEE	UNCATEGORIZED			($350.00)
5/4/2026	OVERDRAFT FEE	UNCATEGORIZED			($105.00)
4/20/2026	FEE FOR ATM WTD 04/19 21:45 FIFTH THIRD BANK ST AUGUSTINE FL FNBF2345 008~6011	ATM			($2.95)
4/20/2026	SURCHARGE FEE 8398 ATM WTD 04/19 21:45 FIFTH THIRD BANK ST AUGUSTINE FL FNBF234	UNCATEGORIZED			($3.50)
4/17/2026	OVERDRAFT FEE	UNCATEGORIZED			($140.00)
4/16/2026	OVERDRAFT FEE	UNCATEGORIZED			($70.00)

Older Transactions

Newer Transactions

https://banking-fnb.fnb-onlinebankingcenter.com/FNBPA/Accounts/PMMActivity.aspx?index=2 2/2

Figure 2. Bank Statement

charges. The following transactions have been recorded against the Account since February 23, 2026, as reflected in the official PNC Online Banking statement attached hereto as Exhibit A:

Date	Description	Amount
02/23/2026	[illegible] — ACH WEB I2Y899JPB	-$132.86
02/23/2026	DEBIT CARD PURCHASE — [illegible]	-$74.34
02/24/2026	OVERDRAFT ITEM FEE	-$36.00
02/24/2026	OVERDRAFT ITEM FEE	-$36.00
03/02/2026	SERVICE CHARGE PERIOD ENDING 02/27/2026	-$12.00
03/02/2026	[illegible] — ACH WEB IZBE5AAKM	-$132.86
03/03/2026	RETURNED ITEM FEE (NSF)	-$36.00
03/03/2026	ZEL FROM [illegible]	+$620.00
03/03/2026	ZEL TO JUAN RODULFO	-$120.00
03/05/2026	DEBIT CARD PURCHASE — [illegible]	-$37.17
03/06/2026	DEBIT CARD PURCHASE — [illegible]	-$37.17
03/06/2026	OVERDRAFT ITEM FEE	-$36.00
03/09/2026	OVERDRAFT ITEM FEE	-$36.00
03/09/2026	ACH DEBIT — [illegible] (Pending)	-$132.86
03/06/2026	[illegible] CARD3411 (Pending)	-$37.17

Total Overdraft and NSF Fees Assessed: $180.00 (overdraft) + $36.00 (NSF) = $216.00
Total Service Charges: $12.00

Figure 3. Bank Statement

Appendix B Demand Letters

FROM: JUAN RODULFO On Behalf of GUARIPETE SOLUTIONS

Kissimmee FL

DATE: May 4, 2026

TO:
PNC Bank, N.A.
Legal Department / Customer Dispute Resolution
One PNC Plaza
249 Fifth Avenue
Pittsburgh, Pennsylvania 15222

RE: FORMAL LEGAL DEMAND FOR REVERSAL OF ALL UNAUTHORIZED AND HARMFUL DEBITS, OVERDRAFT FEES, NSF FEES, AND SERVICE CHARGES — ACCOUNT NO. ENDING IN x2346 — BUSINESS CHECKING ACCOUNT — GUARIPETE SOLUTIONS

VIA CERTIFIED MAIL — RETURN RECEIPT REQUESTED

I. INTRODUCTION AND PARTIES

I, Juan Rodulfo, the authorized owner and representative of GUARIPETE SOLUTIONS, a business holding PNC Business Checking Account No. ending in x2346 ("the Account"), hereby submit this formal legal demand letter to PNC Bank, N.A. ("PNC" or "the Bank"), pursuant to applicable federal and state consumer protection laws, banking regulations, and equitable principles. This letter constitutes a formal and legally binding demand for the immediate reversal and reimbursement of all debits, overdraft fees, non-sufficient funds (NSF) fees, and service charges assessed against the Account since February 23, 2026, along with a demand that the Bank cease and desist from imposing future unauthorized overdraft charges against the Account.

This matter is of utmost urgency. The Bank's actions — specifically, its repeated and cascading imposition of overdraft and NSF fees — have caused severe and irreparable financial harm to GUARIPETE SOLUTIONS, disrupting its business operations and cash flow, and have inflicted substantial emotional and personal distress upon me individually.

II. FACTUAL BACKGROUND

Beginning on February 23, 2026, PNC Bank began processing a series of transactions against the Account that directly resulted in a cascade of overlapping overdraft fees, NSF fees, and service

Figure 4. Demand Letter to PNC Page 1

charges. The following transactions have been recorded against the Account since February 23, 2026, as reflected in the official PNC Online Banking statement attached hereto as Exhibit A:

Date	Description	Amount
02/23/2026	[illegible] — ACH WEB I2Y899JPB	-$132.86
02/23/2026	DEBIT CARD PURCHASE — [illegible]	-$74.34
02/24/2026	OVERDRAFT ITEM FEE	-$36.00
02/24/2026	OVERDRAFT ITEM FEE	-$36.00
03/02/2026	SERVICE CHARGE PERIOD ENDING 02/27/2026	-$12.00
03/02/2026	[illegible]H — ACH WEB IZBE5AAKM	-$132.86
03/03/2026	RETURNED ITEM FEE (NSF)	-$36.00
03/03/2026	ZEL FROM [illegible]	+$620.00
03/03/2026	ZEL TO JUAN RODULFO	-$120.00
03/05/2026	DEBIT CARD PURCHASE — [illegible]	-$37.17
03/06/2026	DEBIT CARD PURCHASE — [illegible]	-$37.17
03/06/2026	OVERDRAFT ITEM FEE	-$36.00
03/09/2026	OVERDRAFT ITEM FEE	-$36.00
03/09/2026	ACH DEBIT — [illegible] (Pending)	-$132.86
03/06/2026	[illegible] CARD3411 (Pending)	-$37.17

Total Overdraft and NSF Fees Assessed: $180.00 (overdraft) + $36.00 (NSF) = $216.00
Total Service Charges: $12.00

Figure 5. Demand Letter to PNC Page 2

Total Fees Subject to Immediate Demand: $228.00
Total All Debits Since February 23, 2026 (including all charges): $837.43

III. THE CRITICAL AND PIVOTAL ZELLE PAYMENT OF MARCH 3, 2026

On March 3, 2026, a Zelle electronic payment in the amount of **$620.00** was received into the Account from customer ("the $620.00 Payment"). This payment represented a legitimate and lawful business receipt that, if properly credited and applied by the Bank without interference, would have — and should have — provided sufficient available funds to cover pending transactions and prevent any further overdraft activity.

Despite the receipt of this $620.00 payment, PNC Bank continued to impose overdraft fees on subsequent transaction dates of March 6 and March 9, 2026, compounding the already devastating financial injury caused by earlier fees. The Bank's failure to properly recognize the available balance resulting from the $620.00 Zelle payment, and its continued imposition of overdraft fees thereafter, constitutes a material breach of its obligations and duties to this Account holder.

It is axiomatic that a banking institution cannot, in good conscience and in compliance with applicable law, continue to assess punitive overdraft fees upon a business account that has received a bona fide deposit sufficient to restore a positive balance. PNC's conduct in this regard is not merely inappropriate — it is legally actionable.

IV. LEGAL BASIS FOR THIS DEMAND

PNC Bank's conduct described herein violates multiple provisions of federal and state law, as well as the Bank's own contractual obligations, including but not limited to:

A. Breach of Contract and Duty of Good Faith and Fair Dealing

The Account Agreement between GUARIPETE SOLUTIONS and PNC Bank constitutes a binding contract. The implied covenant of good faith and fair dealing, recognized under applicable contract law, prohibits a contracting party from acting in a manner that deprives the other party of the benefit of the bargain. PNC's repeated imposition of cascading overdraft fees — particularly following the receipt of a $620.00 Zelle deposit — constitutes a material breach of this duty.

B. Unfair, Deceptive, or Abusive Acts or Practices (UDAAP)

Under the Dodd-Frank Wall Street Reform and Consumer Protection Act (12 U.S.C. § 5531 et seq.) and the Consumer Financial Protection Bureau's (CFPB) implementing regulations, financial institutions are prohibited from engaging in unfair, deceptive, or abusive acts or practices. The imposition of multiple cascading overdraft fees — particularly when a substantial

Figure 6. Demand Letter to PNC Page 3

deposit has been received — constitutes an "unfair" practice under 12 U.S.C. § 5531(c), as it causes substantial injury that is not reasonably avoidable and is not outweighed by any countervailing benefit.

C. Regulation E — Electronic Fund Transfers Act (12 C.F.R. Part 1005)

Under Regulation E and the Electronic Fund Transfers Act (15 U.S.C. § 1693 et seq.), financial institutions must ensure that the posting of electronic fund transfers — including Zelle payments — is handled in a manner consistent with consumer protection standards. The failure to properly apply the $620.00 Zelle credit to prevent subsequent overdraft fee assessments implies the Bank's obligations under this regulatory framework.

D. CFPB Overdraft Rule and Supervisory Guidance

The CFPB has repeatedly issued guidance and supervisory findings confirming that excessive and cascading overdraft fees constitute an abusive practice. Multiple enforcement actions have been taken against large financial institutions — including those similarly situated to PNC — for precisely the type of conduct described herein. PNC is on notice of these regulatory expectations.

E. Unfair and Deceptive Trade Practices Under State Law

Under the applicable state consumer protection statutes, including but not limited to the Pennsylvania Unfair Trade Practices and Consumer Protection Law (73 P.S. § 201-1 et seq.), unfair and deceptive banking practices that cause financial and emotional harm to consumers are actionable. This letter hereby places PNC on notice that all available state law remedies are preserved and will be pursued if this matter is not resolved promptly.

F. Emotional Distress and Personal Harm

The cumulative effect of PNC's repeated, overlapping, and cascading overdraft fees has caused me, Juan Rodulfo, severe emotional distress, anxiety, and personal hardship. As a small business owner, the financial stability of GUARIPETE SOLUTIONS is directly intertwined with my personal well-being and livelihood. The Bank's actions have disrupted my ability to meet business obligations, pay vendors, serve customers, and maintain the dignity of my commercial enterprise. This harm is real, documented, and compensable.

V. ITEMIZED DEMAND FOR RELIEF

Based on the foregoing, I hereby formally demand that PNC Bank, N.A., take the following actions **within ten (10) business days** of receipt of this letter:

1. **Immediate Full Reversal** of all Overdraft Item Fees assessed since February 23, 2026, totaling **$216.00** ($36.00 × 6 instances);

Figure 7. Demand Letter to PNC Page 4

2. **Immediate Full Reversal** of the Service Charge assessed on March 2, 2026, in the amount of **$12.00**, for the period ending February 27, 2026;

3. **Immediate Reversal** of all other debits posted to the Account since February 23, 2026, that directly resulted in or contributed to the overdraft condition, as itemized in Section II above;

4. **Restoration of the Account to a positive standing** sufficient to reflect the proper available balance that would have existed but for the Bank's improper fee assessments;

5. **Cancellation and block of all pending overdraft fee assessments**, including any fees anticipated in connection with the pending[redacted]H (-$132.86) and the pendin[redacted]CARD3411 (-$37.17);

6. **Formal written confirmation** that the Account will NOT be subjected to future unauthorized overdraft charges without the explicit, affirmative, written consent of the Account holder, in full compliance with Regulation E opt-in requirements (12 C.F.R. § 1005.17);

7. **A written apology and formal acknowledgment** of the harm caused to GUARIPETE SOLUTIONS and to me personally by the Bank's conduct; and

8. **Preservation of all records** related to this Account, including but not limited to all transaction records, posting sequences, overdraft processing procedures, and fee assessment records from January 1, 2026, through the present, in anticipation of potential litigation.

VI. NOTICE OF INTENT TO ESCALATE

If PNC Bank fails to respond affirmatively and substantively to this demand within **ten (10) business days** of receipt of this letter, I hereby provide notice of my intent to:

a. File a formal complaint with the **Consumer Financial Protection Bureau (CFPB)** at consumerfinance.gov;

b. File a formal complaint with the **Office of the Comptroller of the Currency (OCC)**;

c. File a formal complaint with the **Pennsylvania Department of Banking and Securities**;

d. Pursue all available civil remedies in a court of competent jurisdiction, including but not limited to claims for breach of contract, breach of the implied covenant of good faith and fair dealing, violation of UDAAP, and emotional distress damages;

e. Seek an award of attorneys' fees and costs to the full extent permitted by applicable law; and

Figure 8. Demand Letter to PNC Page 5

f. Consider escalating this matter to media and consumer advocacy organizations to bring public attention to PNC Bank's overdraft fee practices.

VII. CONCLUSION

I have been a customer of PNC Bank and have entrusted the Bank with the financial operations of GUARIPETE SOLUTIONS. The Bank's repeated and cascading imposition of overdraft and NSF fees — particularly in the face of a $620.00 Zelle payment that should have restored the Account's positive standing — has been nothing short of devastating to my business and to me personally. I urge PNC Bank to do the right thing: reverse these charges, restore the Account, and commit to treating this customer with the fairness, dignity, and legal compliance that federal and state law demand.

I await your prompt and substantive written response no later than **May 23, 2026**.

Respectfully submitted,

JUAN RODULFO
Authorized Representative, GUARIPETE SOLUTIONS
Account No. Ending x2346
Date: March 9, 2026
Email: [redacted]@rodulfox.com

Enclosures:
- Exhibit A: PNC Online Banking Transaction Statement — GUARIPETE SOLUTIONS x2346 (February 23, 2026 – March 9, 2026)

Figure 9. Demand Letter to PNC Page 6

First National Bank of Pennsylvania
Attn: Customer Advocacy / Dispute Resolution Department
4140 E. State Street
Hermitage, PA 16148

Date: May 2, 2026

Re: Formal Demand for Reimbursement of Overdraft (NSF) Fees and Cease of Overdraft Authorization
Account Holder: GUARIPETE SOLUTIONS, INC
Authorized Signer: Juan R. Rodulfo
Account Number: ****1751

To Whom It May Concern:

I represent the above-referenced account holder and hereby submit a formal dispute and demand for the immediate reimbursement of all overdraft/non-sufficient funds ("NSF") fees assessed on the account from January 1, 2026 through the present date, including any pending transactions.

SPECIFIC DISPUTED CHARGES

The following overdraft fees have been identified and are hereby formally disputed:

- May 2026 (Pending): "PROCESSING: OVERDRAFT FEE" — $105.00
- March 9, 2026: "OVERDRAFT FEE" — $35.00
- April 16, 2026: "OVERDRAFT FEE" — $70.00
- April 17, 2026: "OVERDRAFT FEE" — $140.00

Total Amount in Dispute: **$350.00**

These charges, individually and collectively, constitute an excessive and unjustified financial burden on the account holder.

LEGAL BASIS FOR DISPUTE

This demand is grounded in applicable federal regulations and consumer protection principles, including but not limited to:

1. **Regulation E (12 C.F.R. § 1005.17)** – To the extent overdraft fees were imposed on ATM or one-time debit card transactions, such fees are only permissible upon clear, affirmative, and informed opt-in by the account holder. You are hereby requested to provide documentary evidence of such consent.

Figure 10. Demand Letter to FNB Page 1

2. **Unfair, Deceptive, or Abusive Acts or Practices (UDAAP)** – The repeated imposition of overdraft fees—particularly in connection with low-dollar transactions and transaction posting practices—may constitute unfair or abusive conduct under federal law.

3. **Duty of Good Faith and Fair Dealing** – The systematic assessment of disproportionate fees, especially where account balances fluctuate due to timing of deposits and withdrawals, violates the reasonable expectations of fair banking practices.

DAMAGES AND HARM

The overdraft fees assessed have caused significant and ongoing harm, including:

- Severe disruption to the cash flow and operational stability of GUARIPETE SOLUTIONS, INC.;
- Artificial inflation of negative balances due solely to fee accumulation;
- Emotional distress, anxiety, and personal hardship experienced by the account holder;
- Adverse impact on the ability to maintain ordinary business transactions.

These damages are direct, foreseeable, and attributable to the pattern of fee imposition.

FORMAL DEMANDS

Accordingly, we hereby demand that First National Bank of Pennsylvania:

1. **Immediately reimburse the full amount of $350.00**, representing all overdraft/NSF fees assessed from January 2026 to date, including pending charges;
2. Provide a **complete written accounting** of all overdraft-related charges, including the triggering transactions and internal fee assessment methodology;
3. Provide **documentary proof of valid opt-in consent** for overdraft services, if any exists;
4. **Immediately revoke and disable any overdraft protection or authorization**, and place the account in a "decline-only" status to prevent any future overdraft transactions;
5. Confirm in writing that **no further overdraft or NSF fees will be assessed** absent explicit, renewed, and documented authorization.

NOTICE OF INTENT TO ESCALATE

If First National Bank of Pennsylvania fails to respond affirmatively and substantively to this demand within **ten (10) business days** of receipt of this letter, I hereby provide notice of my intent to:

Figure 11. Demand Letter to FNB Page 2

a. File a formal complaint with the **Consumer Financial Protection Bureau (CFPB)** at consumerfinance.gov;

b. File a formal complaint with the **Office of the Comptroller of the Currency (OCC)**;

c. File a formal complaint with the **Pennsylvania Department of Banking and Securities**;

d. Pursue all available civil remedies in a court of competent jurisdiction, including but not limited to claims for breach of contract, breach of the implied covenant of good faith and fair dealing, violation of UDAAP, and emotional distress damages;

e. Seek an award of attorneys' fees and costs to the full extent permitted by applicable law; and

f. Consider escalating this matter to media and consumer advocacy organizations to bring public attention to First National Bank of Pennsylvania's overdraft fee practices.

This correspondence is submitted without prejudice to any rights, claims, or causes of action, all of which are expressly reserved.

I await your prompt and substantive written response no later than **May 23, 2026**.

Respectfully submitted,

Juan R. Rodulfo
Authorized Representative
GUARIPETE SOLUTIONS, INC

Kissimmee, FL
Email: @rodulfox.com
Phone:

Figure 12. Demand Letter to FNB Page 3

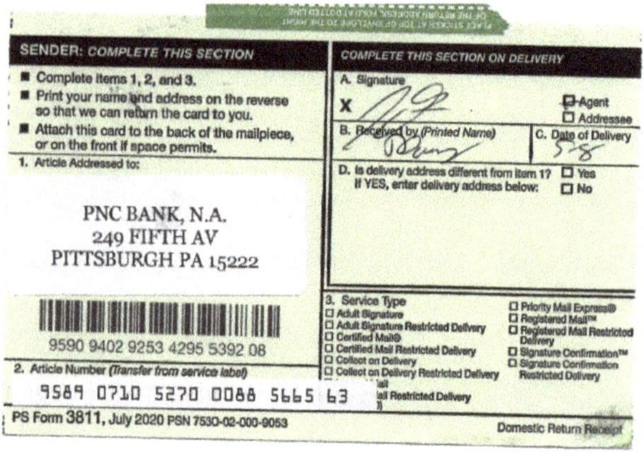

SENDER: COMPLETE THIS SECTION

- Complete items 1, 2, and 3.
- Print your name and address on the reverse so that we can return the card to you.
- Attach this card to the back of the mailpiece, or on the front if space permits.

1. Article Addressed to:

PNC BANK, N.A.
249 FIFTH AV
PITTSBURGH PA 15222

9590 9402 9253 4295 5392 08

2. Article Number (Transfer from service label)

9589 0710 5270 0088 5665 63

COMPLETE THIS SECTION ON DELIVERY

A. Signature X ☑ Agent ☐ Addressee

B. Received by (Printed Name) C. Date of Delivery 5-8

D. Is delivery address different from item 1? ☐ Yes
If YES, enter delivery address below: ☐ No

3. Service Type
☐ Adult Signature
☐ Adult Signature Restricted Delivery
☐ Certified Mail®
☐ Certified Mail Restricted Delivery
☐ Collect on Delivery
☐ Collect on Delivery Restricted Delivery
☐ Priority Mail Express®
☐ Registered Mail™
☐ Registered Mail Restricted Delivery
☐ Signature Confirmation™
☐ Signature Confirmation Restricted Delivery

PS Form 3811, July 2020 PSN 7530-02-000-9053 Domestic Return Receipt

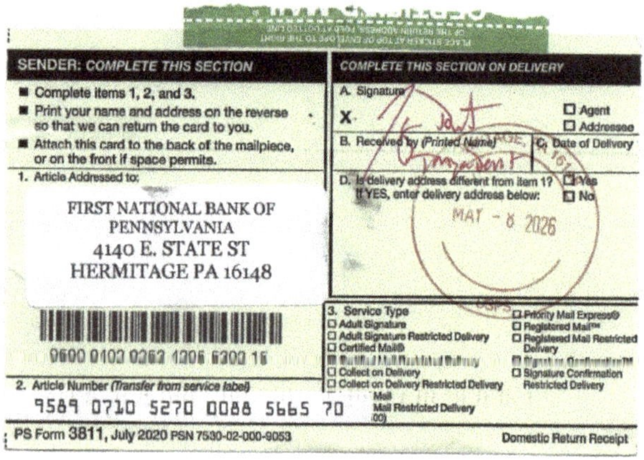

SENDER: COMPLETE THIS SECTION

- Complete items 1, 2, and 3.
- Print your name and address on the reverse so that we can return the card to you.
- Attach this card to the back of the mailpiece, or on the front if space permits.

1. Article Addressed to:

FIRST NATIONAL BANK OF PENNSYLVANIA
4140 E. STATE ST
HERMITAGE PA 16148

9590 9402 9253 4295 5392 15

2. Article Number (Transfer from service label)

9589 0710 5270 0088 5665 70

COMPLETE THIS SECTION ON DELIVERY

A. Signature X ☐ Agent ☐ Addressee

B. Received by (Printed Name) C. Date of Delivery

D. Is delivery address different from item 1? ☐ Yes
If YES, enter delivery address below: ☐ No

MAY - 8 2026

3. Service Type
☐ Adult Signature
☐ Adult Signature Restricted Delivery
☐ Certified Mail®
☐ Certified Mail Restricted Delivery
☐ Collect on Delivery
☐ Collect on Delivery Restricted Delivery
☐ Priority Mail Express®
☐ Registered Mail™
☐ Registered Mail Restricted Delivery
☐ Signature Confirmation™
☐ Signature Confirmation Restricted Delivery

PS Form 3811, July 2020 PSN 7530-02-000-9053 Domestic Return Receipt

Figure 13. USPS Domestic Return Receipts

Appendix C Bank Responses

On Wednesday, May 20th, 2026 at 08:37 <@pnc.com> wrote:

Dear Juan Rodulfio,

Connecting with our customers is very important to us. A concern was recently brought to the attention of PNC Bank Executive Client Relations, for priority handling and oversight. I would appreciate the opportunity to discuss your concerns.

My office hours are Monday-Friday, 8:00 a.m. – 5:00 p.m. Eastern Time. You may reach me at 26

Please be advised that this is an unsecured form of communication. In efforts to protect your privacy respond only with general information.

I look forward to speaking with you.

Sincerely,

s (he/him/his)

Executive Client Relations

PNC-Certified Women's Business Advocate

PNC Bank

(P): 2

(F): 84

@pnc.com

PNC BANK

Figure 14. Email from PNC offering a discussion over the phone

Re: PNC Concern

From Guaripete Solutions @rodulfox.com>
To @pnc.com>
Date Wednesday, May 20th, 2026 at 11:25

Dear Mr.

I acknowledge receipt of your email. As stated in my formal legal demand sent to PNC Bank via certified mail, all communications regarding this matter must be conducted **strictly in writing**. This requirement is intentional, necessary, and non-negotiable.

Given the legal nature of the dispute, the documented financial harm to my business, and the need to preserve all records for potential regulatory and judicial review, I will not engage in telephone discussions. Written communication ensures accuracy, transparency, and a verifiable record of all representations made by PNC Bank.

Accordingly, please provide the following **in writing**:

1. Confirmation that PNC has opened a formal investigation into the overdraft and NSF fee assessments detailed in my certified demand letter.
2. The name, title, and department of the individual(s) assigned to the investigation.
3. A written explanation of the scope of your review, including whether PNC is examining posting order, ledger balance vs. available balance discrepancies, and the handling of the March 3rd Zelle deposit.
4. A written timeline for PNC's response and resolution.

Please note that this written-only communication requirement is fully consistent with federal regulatory complaint procedures, CFPB documentation standards, and litigation-preservation protocols.

I will continue to respond promptly to all written correspondence.

Sincerely, Juan Rodulfo, owner of Guaripete Solutions Inc.

Figure 15. Email response (AI Generated) to PNC's email

First National Bank

Charlotte, NC 28216

May 26, 2026

Guaripete Solutions, Inc.
Juan R. Rudolfo

Kissimmee,

Re: Formal Demand for Reimbursement of Overdraft (NSF) Fees and Cease to Overdraft

Dear Mr. Rudolfo,

Please accept this letter in response to the letter that we received from you on May 11, 2026, regarding your business checking account at First National Bank of Pennsylvania (FNB).

We have reviewed the details of your letter regarding Overdraft fees (OD fees). Pursuant to the Deposit Account Agreement (DAA), provided to you at account opening, the relevant portions of which are enclosed for your reference, if your available balance is not sufficient to pay all of your transactions that present to your account, FNB will either pay the transaction into overdraft or return the transaction as unpaid. When a transaction is paid into overdraft, your account may be charged an OD fee in accordance with the Business Fee Schedule, which is enclosed for your reference. Please note that all business accounts are opted-in to Overdraft Services (ODS) and only consumer accounts must have the option to opt-out under Regulation E. Opting in to ODS may pay a transaction into overdraft if it presents to your account against an insufficient balance.

Only you as the account owner have full knowledge of all debits and credits being presented to your checking account. It is your responsibility to balance your checking account and to know your available balance by recording all credits and debits in your checkbook, or by reviewing Mobile Banking or Online Banking. Any transaction we receive as posted, pending or preauthorized to your account will affect your available balance. Your available balance does not include any checks you may have written, or electronic Automatic Clearing House transactions (ACH) that you have scheduled which have not posted to your checking account.

On March 5, 2026, the ending balance for your checking account was negative $13.08. Although the $11.81 transaction caused your account to become overdrawn on this day, an OD fee was not assessed because there were sufficient funds in the account when the transaction was initiated. To determine your available balance, we take your ending balance from the prior business day plus or minus any preauthorized debits or available credits. Your available balance to pay items on March 6, 2026, was $30.64, because six (6) credits posted to your account totaling $61.04, and two (2) preauthorized debits were pending totaling $17.32. From your available balance, your account was presented with three (3) items totaling $36.24, which posted to your account leaving a negative balance of $5.60. The OD fee assessed to your account on March 9, 2026, totaling $35.00, was caused by the transaction in the amount of $10.40.

Figure 16. Response Letter from FNB Page 1

First National Bank

NC 28216

We have reviewed the overdrafts that occurred on your account and have confirmed that the fees on the following dates were all caused by preauthorized pending activity that reduced your balance to pay transactions: $70.00 on April 16, 2026, $140.00 on April 17, 2026, and $105.00 on May 4, 2026. The enclosed notifications were provided to you regarding the overdrafts that occurred on your account.

Please note that FNB does not charge an OD fee for everyday debit card transactions that are approved with sufficient funds, but post to your account against an insufficient balance per the enclosed DAA. The following transactions listed with their posting date were not charged an OD fee because there were sufficient funds in the account when they were initiated: $8.85, and $0.30 on April 15, 2026, $128.00 on April 16, 2026, and $26.72 and $ 13.19 on May 4, 2026.

In addition to these items, no fees were charged for the transactions in the amounts of $4.55, $3.58, and $1.99 on May 4, 2026, because FNB does not apply OD fees for transactions that cause an overdraft but are in the amount of $5.00 or less.

As of the date of this letter, your account remains overdrawn and continues to accrue OD fees and Continuous Overdraft fees in accordance with the Business Fee Schedule. We encourage you to bring your account current as soon as possible in order to prevent your account from becoming charged off. Beginning on May 12, 2026, Branch Manager of the Mountain Island Office, began contacting you via phone to discuss your concerns but has been unable to successfully reach you. Please contact him directly at 704 if you have any additional questions or concerns.

FNB recommends reviewing our Financial Insights video about managing your checking account. The enclosed instructions will help to locate this and other helpful videos to manage your account and increase your financial management knowledge.

We hope this response to your complaint meets your satisfaction. While this communication is intended to present the facts of the situation, we would like to express our appreciation for your business and our hope that you will continue to allow us to serve your financial needs.

Sincerely,

Market Manager
Charlotte-Uptown Region
First National Bank

Enclosures

Figure 17. Response Letter from FNB Page 2

www.ingramcontent.com/pod-product-compliance
Lightning Source LLC
LaVergne TN
LVHW050922210926
848482LV00012B/504
* 9 7 9 8 2 4 0 9 3 8 5 4 2 *